NATIONAL GEOGRAPHIC

The Eiffel Tower

Rachel Griffiths

Have you seen this tower before?
It is the Eiffel Tower in Paris, France.
It is one of the most famous towers in the world.

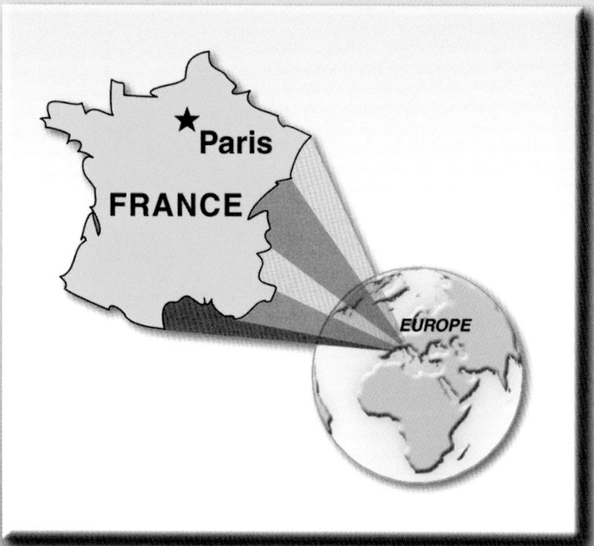

The Eiffel Tower was built for a **fair** that was held in Paris in 1889. A man named Gustave Eiffel **designed** and built the tower. The Eiffel Tower was named after him.

Gustave Eiffel

Math Matters

It took almost two years to build the Eiffel Tower. Work began in April 1887 and ended in March 1889. How many months did it take to build the last 574 feet of the tower?

April 1887
Work begins.

January 1888
180 feet

July 1888
348 feet

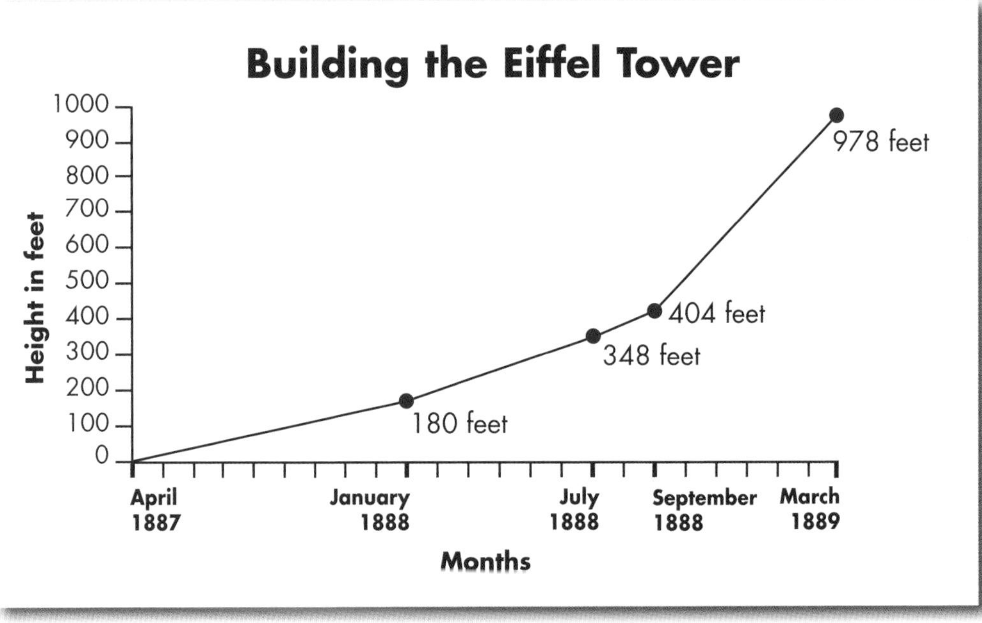

September 1888
404 feet

March 1889
978 feet

Gustave Eiffel made the tower out of a strong metal called **iron**. He arranged the iron beams in a pattern of triangles. The triangle shapes helped make the tower strong, too.

GODIN
DE DION

Math Matters

How do the triangles help make the Eiffel Tower strong? A triangle is a really strong shape. It's much stronger than a square.

A Test of Strength

If you push on a square, like this, it will lose its shape.

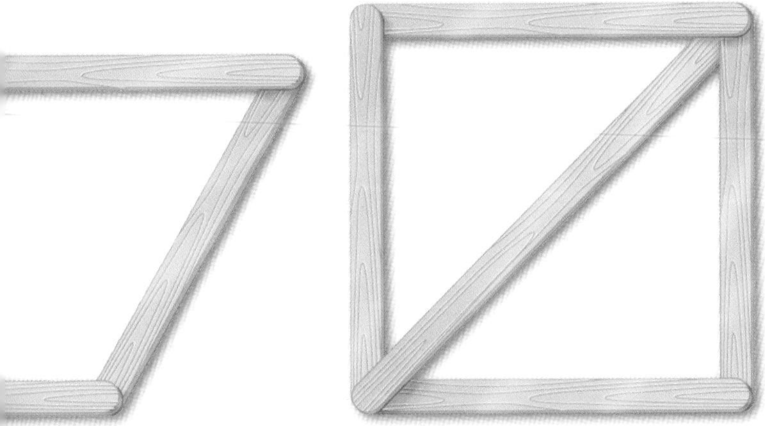

You can make the square stronger by adding a brace. The brace makes two triangle shapes.

Because the iron triangles were so strong, Gustave Eiffel could make his tower tall. The Eiffel Tower was the tallest building in the world when it was built.

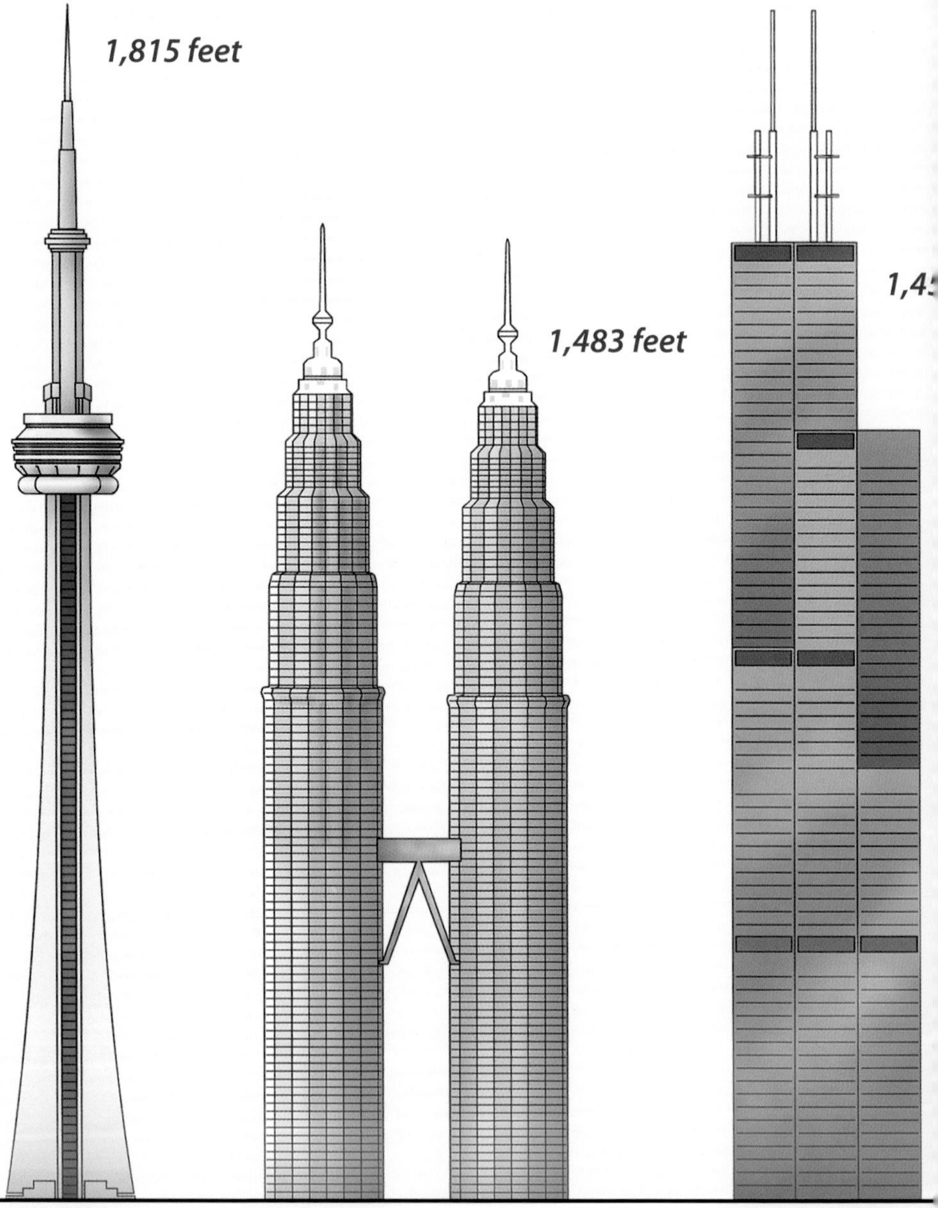

CN Tower
Canada
1976

Petronas Twin Towers
Malaysia
1998

Sears Tower
United States
1974

Math Matters

Today other buildings are much taller than the Eiffel Tower. How much taller are the other buildings?

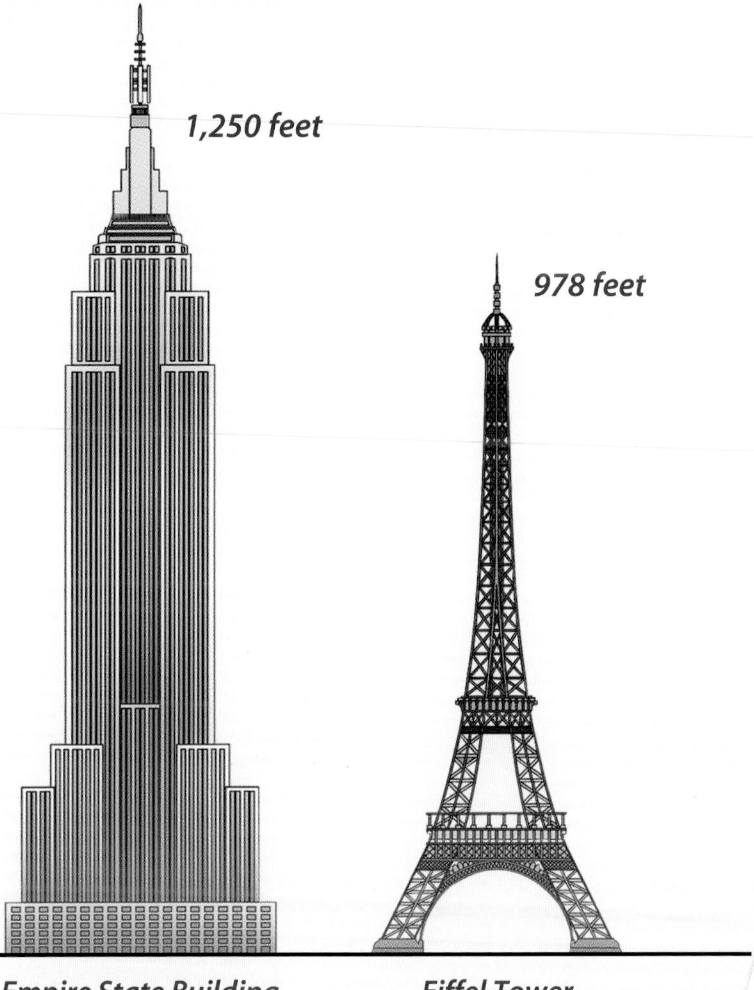

Empire State Building
United States
1931

Eiffel Tower
France
1889

Glossary

design	to make plans or drawings of something
fair	a place to show goods
iron	a strong, heavy metal